My
Animal
Friends

Other Dick King-Smith
books to collect:

Lady Lollipop
Clever Lollipop
The Finger-Eater
Aristotle
The Twin Giants
and
The Sophie Stories

My
Animal
Friends

Thirty-One
True Life Stories

written by
Dick King-Smith

illustrated by
Anita Jeram

WALKER
BOOKS

First published as a picture book in Great Britain 1996
by Walker Books Ltd
87 Vauxhall Walk, London SE11 5HJ

This edition published 2013

2 4 6 8 10 9 7 5 3 1

Text © 1996 Foxbusters Ltd
Illustrations © 1996 Anita Jeram

The right of Dick King-Smith and Anita Jeram to be identified as
author and illustrator of this work has been asserted
by them in accordance with the Copyright, Designs and Patents
Act 1988

This book has been typeset in Stempel Schneidler and Souvenir

Printed and bound in Great Britain by Clays Ltd, St Ives plc

British Library Cataloguing in Publication Data:
A catalogue record for this book is available from
the British Library

ISBN 978-0-7445-9419-5

www.walker.co.uk

For Myrle
D.K-S.

For Deirdre and Lucy
A.J.

Foreword

I THOUGHT I WOULD TELL YOU ABOUT SOME OF MY
ANIMAL FRIENDS.

Ever since I was very little, I've enjoyed
the company of animals, big and small.
I can still remember the thrill of riding on
an elephant at the zoo when
I was four, and the excitement
of getting my first white mice.

As a schoolboy, I was mad on pets, and
even as a wartime soldier I kept
chameleons in North Africa
and a puppy in Italy.

After the war came twenty years
of farming. I was married by then, with
three children, and we lived in the country
surrounded by all sorts of beasts and birds.

Later, as a presenter on children's TV,
I worked with loads of different creatures,

from chickens to chimps,
from pigs to pythons.

It's not surprising that I like to write stories about animals. This is a book of little tales about a few of my animal friends.

Some I was very fond of and knew for the whole of their lives, like Dodo the dachshund or Frank the rabbit.

Some I only had for a very short time, like the golden pheasants.

And some, like the two badgers or Midnight the angry cow, weren't all that friendly to me!

But all were interesting – one way or another – and each was unforgettable. I've enjoyed writing about them.

If you enjoy reading about them, then everyone's happy!

Dick King-Smith

List of Stories

The Elephant Ride

I REMEMBER, WHEN I WAS QUITE SMALL, going for a ride on an elephant at the zoo. I imagined we were in the jungle, and a tiger would appear.

I would be quite safe, of course, on top of the elephant. All the same I think I was quite glad to see my mother appear instead and wave at me.

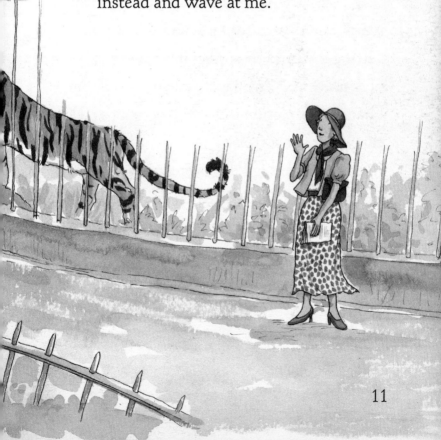

No Luck

WHEN I WAS ABOUT EIGHT, I had a tortoise.

 I didn't know if it was male or female. By day it plodded slowly about on a patch of grass. At night I put an upturned wooden box over it: to keep it warm and dry, to stop it wandering off and getting lost, and to protect it from eagles. (There weren't any eagles where I lived, but I had seen a picture in a story-book of an eagle carrying off a tortoise.)

One morning I discovered that my tortoise was a she. I lifted up the wooden box and there beside her was a little round egg, like a miniature table tennis ball.

I didn't say anything to anyone about the tortoise egg, but took it into our house and upstairs to the airing-cupboard (the hot cupboard, we called it), where sheets and pillowcases and blankets were all laid out, on slatted wooden shelves in the warm darkness. I put my egg carefully between some nice thick blankets.

I wasn't sure how long it took for tortoise eggs to hatch out, so I kept on going to look at it, every day for ages and ages.

I didn't realize you had to have a father tortoise as well as a mother.

Tree Frog

ONCE, LONG AGO, I was
given a green tree frog.
All I can recall about
it is that it was very
small, bright green in
colour, and had suckers
on the ends of its
fingers and toes so that
it could climb up a pane
of glass.

Catching the Skipper

ONE OF MY GRANDFATHERS was a very keen lepidopterist; that's to say someone who collects butterflies and moths. I don't think this happens so much nowadays. I hope not.

He had a beautifully made mahogany cabinet with dozens of slender drawers in it, each containing trays on which the bodies of hundreds of different butterflies and moths were carefully mounted, their wings spread, their colours as in life.

SKIPPERS Hesperiidae ♂ ♂ ♂

He was a very kind and gentle man, my grandfather was. Yet somehow he never appeared worried at the thought of killing all those lovely insects. He caught each one in his butterfly net and then put it in what we called a "stink-bottle", a jar filled with some poisonous stuff which gassed it.

One day he took me with him to try to catch a small brown butterfly called a Lulworth Skipper, so named because it had first been discovered at Lulworth Cove in Dorset. At that time my grandfather had a car

called a Clyno, a dignified sort of machine
that didn't go very fast, especially when
he was driving.

At twenty miles an hour it took an
awfully long time to cover the hundred-odd
miles to Lulworth, and when we arrived at
last and began to comb the steep sides of the
cove, there was no sign of a Lulworth Skipper.

After a couple of hours, just as we were about to give up and start the long, slow journey home, up fluttered a little dingy brown butterfly.

Quickly my grandfather handed me the net (I was a good fifty years younger, so a lot faster than him).

Off I dashed, and swung the net, and caught the Lulworth Skipper.

We came, we saw, we conquered!

A Palace Fit for Mice

I USED TO KEEP MASSES OF PET MICE.. Many of them

I bought from a mouse farm in South Wales, where you could buy more than forty different colours of mice.

I became a member of the National Mouse Club (subscription 7s. 6d. a year – that's about 37p) and I wore a little badge with a picture of a mouse under the letters N.M.C.

But what I liked best about keeping mice was building cages for them. The cages I built were nothing less than mouse-palaces. They were very big, with glass fronts so that I could see my mice running about, and inside there were two floors with

stairs connecting them, and lots of
little walkways and bridges so that
the mice got plenty of exercise; and,
of course, there were cosy sleeping-

boxes in the upstairs part –
bedrooms where mother mice
could have their children (and
a great many children
they had).

Some people
find it restful to watch
fish in a tank. What I liked best was watching
mice in a mouse-palace.

A Short Stay

WHEN I WAS ABOUT FIFTEEN OR SO, I was lucky enough to have a wonderful place to keep some of my pets. It was an unused grass tennis-court, that had been fenced around with chicken-wire, sides and top, to make a huge cage. In it I kept lots of guinea-pigs and rabbits, and a tortoise or two.

One unforgettable day I was given two new pets: a pair of golden pheasants. Like many hen birds (who need to be camouflaged while they're sitting on their eggs), the female golden pheasant is quite a drab colour, a yellowish brown barred with black.

But the male golden pheasant
is a magnificent-looking fellow, with
a very long tail and brilliant feathering
of gold and scarlet. On his head is a
glowing yellow crest and, on his shoulders,
a fiery amber cape or ruff above dark green
patches. You can't imagine a more colourful
bird. This one minced around his mate with
little high-stepping strides, his ruff raised, and
gave a shrill whistle.

You can imagine my feelings of delight
when these pheasants – my pheasants –
arrived that morning.

But you certainly can't imagine what
I felt like later in the day. In the roof of the
wire run there was, unknown to anyone,
a hole where the wire had rusted away. The
golden pheasants found it.

That evening I went to feed them, and
they were no longer there. The rabbits and
the guinea-pigs hopped and scurried about as
usual, and the tortoises slow-marched around,
but the pheasants were gone.

The hen bird had disappeared altogether,
but the cock was sitting in the top of a tall
tree near by, his colours brilliant in the light
of the setting sun. There was nothing I could
do, no possible way of catching him.

I could only stand and
stare. By the morning he'd
gone. I never saw him again.

More and More Rats

NOBODY MUCH LIKES RATS. They are thought of as vicious, cunning, smelly carriers of disease. Pet rats, on the other hand, are very clean and easy to handle, and make fascinating companions.

I know that the pair I once had couldn't have been more likeable. They were Japanese Hooded Rats, pure white on the sides and legs, but with a black head and a black line down the back.

I called them Jupiter and Juno, after a Roman god and goddess. Jupiter was quite a bit bigger than Juno. He was very tame and liked to travel around, sitting on my shoulder. Juno was usually too busy for that sort of thing.

Busy?

Doing what?

Having babies.

In her first litter she had ten cubs. In her
second, twelve.

In her third, sixteen.

What happened

to all those young rats,

I can't remember

– it was so long ago.

But I do remember old

Jupiter very clearly, perched

on my shoulder,

tickling my neck with

his whiskers. He especially

loved digestive biscuits.

Cabbage

ONCE, IN DURBAN, IN SOUTH AFRICA,

I was standing on
the upper deck
of a ship, watching
the cooks chucking
out waste food from the galley
below into the sea. As I watched,
the most enormous shark (I don't
know what sort it was) swam up,
opened its huge mouth and took in
a cabbage. Then it spat it out again.

I don't think it was a vegetarian.

Chameleon-Hunting

BEING BITTEN BY A
CHAMELEON is a funny
feeling. It doesn't
really hurt at all.
It's more of a grip than a bite.
It's as though someone is pinching your finger
with a pair of pliers, but very gently.

Before a chameleon bites you, it threatens
you with a gaping mouth, sometimes hissing
and swaying angrily from side to side.

Once, I had a big cardboard box full of
chameleons, about twelve of them. I'd better
explain, in case you think
that's a cruel way
to keep them.

It was during the Second World War, and we were driving west along the top of Africa, from Cairo all the way to Tripoli. Every evening, when we stopped, I went chameleon-hunting, and I soon filled my box.

I only kept them in it while we were actually travelling. When we stopped, I took them all out and put them on a bush or a low tree branch, so that they could catch flies and other insects, which is what they eat. Just in case they didn't have any luck, I swatted lots of flies and put them in the box.

There was no danger of losing my chameleons.

They moved so slowly that it was a job to catch them at it.

But there's one bit of a chameleon that moves like greased lightning. A chameleon's tongue is as long as its whole body, not counting the tail.

Here's what happens. Chameleons live in trees. They creep along a branch (terribly slowly), holding onto it with their prehensile tails, and with hands and feet that are split so as to grip tightly.

Along comes a fly and settles, so it thinks, well out of chameleon range.

Now the most amazing thing happens. The chameleon's eyes work independently. Each eye is round and bulgy, the eyelids covering most of it, so

that a small hole in
the middle is all the
creature sees with. One
eye can look forward while
the other looks backward.
One can look upward while
the other looks downward.

Back to the fly. There it is, cleaning its
legs perhaps, while the chameleon focuses
on it first with its right eye, then with its left.
Then, like a bolt from the blue, out shoots the

whole length of that clubbed
sticky tongue, and it's
goodbye fly.

Everyone knows the other
thing about the lizards called chameleons.
They can change their colours.

My chameleons stayed mostly brownish
if they were in the cardboard box or sitting
on the knees of my battle-dress trousers.
On bushes they went greenish,
on sand, yellowish.

At night they were usually
cream-coloured with yellow
patches. And when excited,
they turned a sort of reddish-brown with
golden spots. When they were really angry,
those golden spots turned black.

I was fascinated by
them, and I didn't
mind how often
they bit me.

As time went by, they became used to
me and treated me more kindly. Just before we
got to Tripoli, I let them all go. I didn't think
they'd enjoy coming on the invasion of Italy.

I sat watching them move away, very very slowly, into the bushes, hands gripping, feet gripping, tails gripping, eyes swivelling. Somewhere inside each mouth a catapult tongue waited, coiled like a spring.

I watched till every last chameleon was gone from sight.

Killed on Active Service

I HAVE HAD A GREAT NUMBER OF DOGS, many

of whom lived to a good age.
But one died young, killed
on active service.

It was 1943, and we
were fighting our way up
the mountainous west coast of Italy.

Somewhere, in a hilltop village, I came
across this puppy, for that's all she was,
and bought her with a couple of packets
of cigarettes. She was a very Italian-looking
puppy, smooth and slender
and the colour of milky
coffee; a kind
of terrier, but more
whippety. I called
her Vicky.

She travelled with us for some weeks, ate well, and was much spoiled by everyone. Then I had an attack of jaundice and had to go back to Naples, to hospital.

When I got back to the battalion, they told me Vicky had been killed. She'd run across a road straight in front of a lorry. I never saw her grave because we'd moved on, but apparently they'd given her a proper burial and a wooden cross on which was written: VICKY, GRENADIER GUARDS.

Lazy Ben

I ONCE OWNED A BULL NAMED BEN. He was an
Aberdeen Angus, which meant that like all his
breed he was deep-bodied, short-legged and
hornless, with a shiny, satiny, coal-black coat.

Ben was also very lazy. Now you
shouldn't ever trust a bull – of any breed –
but I don't think Ben would have hurt a fly.
It would have been too much effort.

When Ben was in the cowshed, he wore a
stout leather strap around his neck, like a giant
dog collar, with a length of chain fixed to it.

But one fine summer's morning, when the

cows had gone out to grass and Ben was
left alone in his stall, he managed to slip his
head out of the collar. Whose fault it was
I don't remember, but either I or my cowman,
Francis, hadn't done it up tightly enough.

The cowshed had three doors and all
of them were wide open, but Ben couldn't
be bothered to walk as far as the nearest one.

He simply put his head against the
wooden outer wall of the old cowshed,
and pushed.

I know, because I was sweeping the
yard and saw it.

In circuses they used to have dogs that
were trained to jump through paper hoops.
That's what it looked like as, with a loud
splintering noise, first Ben's head and then
his body, came clean through the wall,
with pieces of wood flying everywhere.

Very slowly, so as not to waste energy, Ben ambled into the nearest field and began to graze.

Before I could do anything, I heard a wild shout of anger, and Francis, arriving back from breakfast on his old bicycle, pedalled past me and out into the field.

Throwing down the bike, he ran after Ben, who, alarmed by the angry shouts, began to trot away and even at last to break into a lumbering canter.

Right across the skyline they ran as I watched; but the bull was fat and slow, and the cowman was lean and fast. He soon caught up with Ben.

The last I saw before they disappeared behind a hedge was Francis grabbing hold

of the end of Ben's
tail and pulling back
on it like a man in
a tug-of-war team.

I took the bull-pole and ran to meet
them, but it wasn't needed. Ben was so puffed
out that he couldn't manage more than the
slowest of walks behind Francis, who had one
finger (the little one) crooked through the ring
in the bull's nose.

We tied him up again, making sure
the collar was tight enough, and set about
mending the cowshed wall.

As for Ben, he gave a great sigh and
flopped down, worn out.

Susie

SUSIE WAS A SMALL, HAIRY, BLACK-AND-WHITE TERRILER. I got her from an old chap called Jack

when she was about the size of a guinea-pig. Later, she grew bigger than that, but not much. Susie was always very short-tempered, growling at anyone who said things like, "Get off my chair, Susie."

She loved me best but she growled at me just as much. She followed me everywhere. If I was ploughing, Susie would trot behind the plough in the newly turned furrow, up and down the field, all day long.

During her long life she had numerous brushes with death, but there's one I remember above all the others.

One Boxing Day – a bitterly cold day it was, with a biting east wind – Susie went missing. The days passed with no sign of her, and sadly my wife and I resigned ourselves to the fact that at last her luck had run out.

Eight whole days later, as I came out of the back door of the farmhouse to go and start the morning milking, I saw a filthy, bedraggled little object dragging herself painfully up the yard.

We could only suppose she'd been stuck somewhere deep below ground, and perhaps

had to wait till she became thin enough to struggle free.

To have survived eight days and nights in freezing weather with nothing to eat was just believable, but with nothing to drink? Impossible – for any dog except Susie.

We cleaned her up and fed her on warm milk, glucose and egg, and within a day she was her old self.

We couldn't have been more pleased to have her back, but if Susie was pleased too, she never showed it. She just growled at us, and snarled at all the other dogs as usual.

Badger-Biffing

I BET THERE AREN'T MANY PEOPLE who can say, "Once I biffed a badger on the bottom with my hat."

I can. I was going out early one summer's morning to fetch the cows in for milking. On my way I had to cross a big pasture, and there, right in the middle of it, was a badger.

Now badgers are nocturnal animals and, though there was a big sett in the nearby wood where we often heard them clucking and chattering at night, it wasn't often that we saw them in broad daylight.

So I hurried towards this solitary badger, hoping that it wouldn't run away till I'd had a good look at it. It didn't run away. It didn't take the slightest notice of me, even though I was now standing right beside it. It just carried on snuffling about in the grass.

I felt rather foolish. I took off my hat and biffed the badger gently on its bottom.

It didn't even look up. "What's up with you, my friend?" I said. "You deaf, or blind, or both?"

Slowly, with that rolling bear-like shuffle that badgers have, it began to move towards the wood, while I continued to beat a light tattoo on its backside. Until, at last, it came to a hole in the hedge, and disappeared.

The very next morning I went exactly the same way to fetch the dairy herd, and there, in exactly the same place, were two badgers. My friend, I thought, and his friend!

Happily I ran towards them. With a volley of furious grunts, the two badgers charged at me. I fled at top speed.

Nobody ever believes this story.

But it's true.

Three Special Cats

Dulcie Maude

Jinks

Lupin

Dulcie Maude

OUR FIRST SPECIAL CAT was a tortoiseshell-and-white queen called Dulcie Maude, who had, in her lifetime, one hundred and four kittens.

What's more, she liked to have them in unusual places such as a hay-filled manger in the stables or, on one occasion, in a large cardboard box half full of electric light bulbs.

The most comfortable place that Dulcie Maude ever chose was in a loft where lots of unwanted old things were stored. One of these was a doll's pram that still had its little pillow, blue blankets and pink eiderdown in it.

The doll had long disappeared, but in its place Dulcie Maude lay purring happily in the pram, nursing yet another brood of children.

High Jinks

THE SECOND SPECIAL CAT I remember was a ginger female by the name of Jinks. Jinks lived to be very old – I can't remember how many kittens she had. But I do remember first bringing her home as a kitten

herself. She'd been born in a warehouse and she was really quite wild so, before I took her out of the box I'd carried her home in, I made

sure that the room we were in was escape-proof. I shut the door, closed all the windows

and let Jinks out of the box. It was lucky it was summer and there was no fire in the grate, because

the kitten dashed straight up the chimney.
What wasn't so lucky was that the chimney
needed sweeping, and down came an
avalanche of soot. By the time I'd managed
to reach up inside the chimney and grab hold
of the kitten, I was covered
in the stuff.

As for Jinks, she had
changed colour completely,
from ginger to coal-black.

Loving Lupin

THE THIRD OF MY SPECIAL CATS was another ginger – long-haired this time and a tom. His name was Lupin and in fact he belonged to one of our daughters. But when she and her family went to live in America for a year, Lupin came to stay with us.

Lupin was special because he was in some ways more dog than cat. He bossed our dogs about, and when we took them for walks, Lupin would come too, marching along behind, waving his plumy tail.

And there was another way in which he was different.

Most cats like to keep themselves to themselves, accepting admiration and affection from their owners but not giving much back. Lupin was very loving. He would rub his big round furry face on ours, purring like a steam-engine and making quite a fuss of us.

But we were only the cat-sitters. When his real owner came back after that year in America, you should have seen the fuss that Lupin made of her.

Talk about true love!

Nanny Anna

PEOPLE THINK THAT A DACHSHUND is just a sort of short-legged, long-bodied dog. They do not realize that there are dogs ... and there are dachshunds.

Dogs like to please their owners by doing what they are told. Dachshunds like to please themselves.

Our first ever dachshund was called Anna, and when we got her as a puppy, she took not the slightest notice of anything we said to her.

"She must be stone deaf," we said. But she wasn't. She was just a dachshund.

Apart from being as stubborn as all her breed, Anna's speciality was mother-love. Quite early in her life she began to be called Nanny.

It wasn't just her own puppies that she fussed over. She did not need to be in milk, she just came into it at the drop of a baby. Kittens were well received if there was a cat crisis. And once she tried to play mother to four piglets.

A young sow had rejected them, but Nanny thought that they were lovely and immediately settled down to nurse them in her basket. Alas, newborn piglets, unlike puppies, have sharp little teeth, but still Anna put up with them till they could be fostered on to another sow. She saved their lives, in fact.

The Pig Harness

THE FIRST PIG I EVER OWNED was a pedigree
Large White called Molly. Molly was not only
beautiful and intelligent (as all pigs are), but
very sensible and easy-going.

At that time I only had one old pigsty,
and I didn't like to see her confined in it –
I wanted her to have more freedom. Equally,
I didn't want to spend a lot of money on pig-
fencing. Looking in a farming magazine, I hit
on the solution: a "pig harness".

I sent off for it.

The harness consisted of stout leather straps that buckled round the pig's body, and were then attached to a length of chain that looked strong enough to anchor the *QE2*.

The chain ended in a huge expanding spring, and the spring was fixed to a great steel spike that was driven deep into the ground with a sledgehammer.

Once harnessed, the pig could then move freely in a large circle around the spike, so far but no further. With help, I fixed the straps around Molly's large white body. She stood patiently for the fitting, her attention held by a trough full of food.

Then the harness was attached to the chain, which was attached to the spike.

Her food finished, Molly moved slowly off in her new outfit, until at last she reached the full limit of the chain and came to a full stop. She grunted, and strained against this mysterious thing that was holding her back.

"No use trying to bust that, old girl," I said. "That spike and that spring and that chain would hold an elephant." Molly's reply was a loud squeal of anger. Then she pitted all her strength against the pig harness.

The spike held firm.

The spring, now fully expanded, held.

The chain held.

But suddenly all the stout leather straps and buckles burst apart, and Molly trotted happily away!

Midnight

I ONCE BOUGHT A BLACK COW, the blackest cow you ever saw, coal-black, raven-black, black as midnight (which is what I called her).

Sharp and curved were Midnight's horns, and seeing her in the sale ring I was reminded of pictures of the fighting bulls of Spain.

For some strange reason she went very cheap, and I was pleased with my bargain when the haulier delivered her in time for the afternoon milking.

What a milking that was.

At the first touch of the first cup on the first teat, Midnight exploded into a burst of kicking that stripped the milking machine into its component parts and left me battered, bruised and breathless.

The sheer ferocity of the animal was frightening: she leaped and pranced and bawled in anger. Her fierce eyes blazed and there was no doubt about what she would have done with those twin daggers on her head if the neckchain hadn't restrained her.

A few days later she charged my wife, who had to get under a fence in a great hurry.

"What happened?" I said.

"She put her head down and started to paw at the ground, and then she gave a horrible kind of roar and came straight for me."

"She'll have to go," I said.

She went.

Tortoise-Riding

LOTS OF PEOPLE, INCLUDING ME, can say they've fallen off a horse at some time. But how many can say (as I can), "I've fallen off a tortoise"?

It was, of course, a giant tortoise.

Most giant tortoises live in the Galápagos Islands, in the Pacific. Actually, the tortoise I was riding was not from the Galápagos, but from an island in the Indian Ocean called Aldabra.

I'm not sure which tortoise is the bigger – the Aldabra or the Galápagos – but this one was certainly big enough.

I sat astride its huge, shiny shell, and said, "Gee-up!"

Nothing happened.

Then, with a sudden lurch, the tortoise took a large step forward.

I fell off backwards and landed on my bottom with a bump.

Alas, Poor Evil

MY BROTHER ONCE HAD A FERRET called Evil. Evil was a hob (a male ferret), his long snaky body the usual dirty yellow colour, his eyes pink. Despite his name, he was quite good-natured with people he knew. But one fine day Evil somehow escaped from his hutch and went missing. A search was mounted, but there was no sign of the ferret.

Later, a friend of my brother's called Jeff was rummaging about in a shed, looking for something or other, when, under a pile of old rubbish, he came upon Evil, and grabbed hold of him.

Evil was not best pleased.

He bit deep into the ball of Jeff's thumb.

That evening (the ferret now safely back in his hutch) Jeff went to his doctor for an injection. His mind was full of thoughts of blood-poisoning or even rabies, leading to a painful death.

In fact he suffered no ill effects.

But that night Evil died.

Goats on the Bed

I USED TO KNOW SOME PEOPLE who kept a lot
of goats. They lived in a bungalow (the people,
I mean, not the goats).

One day, on my way to visit them in their
garden, I walked past their bedroom window
and happened to look in. There, lying happily
on the bed, chewing the cud, were two large
nanny-goats.

I mentioned this to the people.

"Oh no!" they said. "Crumbs in the bed
are bad enough, but goats' droppings are
the limit!"

Tree Fox

Not far from the cottage
where we live now is a long, narrow
spinney, threaded by a small stream.

My wife and I were walking along the
edge of it one late September morning when
we saw a fox – a dog fox by the size of him –
slip into the far end of the spinney.

When we entered by the same gap,
we were surprised to see no sign of him;
and though our three dachshunds
– Dodo, Poppy and Little Elsie –
marked his line eagerly, they
lost scent and interest
a little way in.

70

This scene was replayed
on several walks, and always the
dogs lost the scent at the same place,
beneath a big old crack-willow. As
such trees often do, it leaned out over
the stream, its thick trunk at an angle
of forty-five degrees to the ground.
We never found an earth in the
spinney, so always presumed that
the dog fox, on hearing or scenting
us, simply slid out on the far side
and away. Till one day, standing
beneath the willow, we chanced
to look upwards.

There he sat in a comfortable
crotch fifteen feet up, paws together,
brush curled neatly round him, ears
pricked, looking down on us.

What a patronising look it was.

We left, feeling small.

Walking Frank

 I'VE OWNED DOZENS AND DOZENS OF RABBITS, of many different breeds, but Frank is the one I'll always remember best. He was a French Lop, a very big kind of rabbit with drooping ears. In colour he was what's known as a Butterfly Smut – whitish, with lots of brown spots and patches, and on the muzzle a butterfly -shaped marking.

At the time I also had a number of Dutch does, quite small black-and-white rabbits, and Frank became the father of the oddest collection of children.

Some were black-and-white, some brown-and-white, some had smuts on their noses, some didn't. Some had sticking-up ears, some had hanging-down ears, and some had one ear up and one ear down.

Frank loved his food. I weighed him once when he was in his prime and he tipped the scales at eight kilos. He was so big that I knocked three hutches together so that he didn't feel cramped.

I used to exercise
him too, on a collar and
lead. Frank liked these
walks. Often he'd suddenly
do a great buck-jump in the air
to show his pleasure. The problem
was that, though taking a dog for a walk
means that the dog goes where you want,
taking a rabbit for a walk means going
wherever the rabbit chooses.

And Frank always chose the
vegetable garden.

Leslie

DRIVING HOME ONE NIGHT, we saw, in the headlights of the car, a hedgehog in the middle of the road. The lights and the sound of the approaching car had caused it to roll up into a ball.

Hedgehogs have it firmly in their minds that if they're rolled up, they're safe. They may be safe from some predators, but not from cars or lorries.

I picked up this hedgehog in a bit of old rag, and we took him home. Or we took her home; we couldn't tell. So we called him, or her, Leslie, a name that serves for a boy or a girl.

Leslie spent that night in a spare rabbit-hutch, and by the next morning was quite

ready to have a good drink and a meal
of tinned dog-meat, which hedgehogs like
very much.

For several days we kept him or her,
hoping that if he or she got used to us, he or
she might stay when we released him or her
into our garden. Hedgehogs are very useful in
gardens because they eat slugs and snails.

One evening we gave Leslie a last good
meal, then put him or her down on the lawn
and watched as he or she trotted away. Ours
is a walled garden. What we didn't know then
was that hedgehogs are good at climbing walls.

We never saw Leslie again.

Bribery

I WAS ONCE ALLOWED TO HOLD a baby female chimpanzee in a safari park. I sat on a bench, and she sat on my knee, put her arms around my neck and gave me some rubbery kisses.

We were getting on really well together until the little chimp spotted Dodo, my miniature red wire-haired dachshund, who was underneath the bench. The chimp reached down a long arm, and I could see her thinking – I'm going to pull that dog's hair.

Dodo flinched
away, and I could
see her thinking – that
creature is going to pull my hair.

The chimp pulled Dodo's hair.

Luckily I had come prepared for naughty
behaviour. I took a packet of Polo mints out
of my pocket and the chimpanzee instantly
forgot all about the dog. She took each
mint from me delicately between thumb
and forefinger, popped it into her mouth,
crunched, swallowed, and held out her hand
politely for more.

How I would have loved
to take her home with me.

How unhappy Dodo
would have been.

Eric

ONCE I CARRIED AN INDIAN PYTHON draped around my neck, for about half an hour. His name was Eric.

Eric was not a really big python. At his thickest part he was about as thick as a man's thigh, and he was about ten feet in length. Some pythons can be more than twice as long as this. People think that snakes are cold and slimy. Eric's skin was warm and dry, and it was easy to feel the power of the thousands of muscles in his beautifully marked body.

I wore him around my
neck and shoulders like
a giant scarf, and he was
heavy, I can tell you. But
he behaved perfectly, and
I didn't feel the least bit nervous of him.

Except perhaps towards the end of our
meeting, when Eric began to feel he'd had
enough.

At least I think that's what he was trying
to say when he started to squeeze my neck,
just a little.

I handed him back to his keeper.

The Hitch-Hiker

WE WERE ONCE DRIVING
TO WEST WALES, at the start
of a family seaside holiday,
when we saw something
very small and yellow
waddling along the middle
of the road in front of us.

It was a duckling.

It was quite alone, and appeared
determined to go to the seaside, too.

So we gave it a lift and
some chocolate cake.

And afterwards
we brought
it home.

Solomon and Albert

I ONCE KNEW A LLAMA THAT HATED A ZEBRA. Or was it a zebra that hated a llama? I'm not sure. All I know is that they were not the best of friends.

They lived in adjoining paddocks in a private collection of animals, separated by a high chain-link fence. On one side was Albert the llama, and on the other was Solomon the zebra. Every day they would put on the same performance, just like actors in a long-running play.

First, Albert would come up to the wire and stick his head over it, and he would stare at Solomon with that sneering, toothy, condescending stare that llamas have.

Solomon would notice, of course, though he pretended not to. All the time he'd be grazing his way gradually over towards Albert.

Eventually Solomon would come close enough for Albert to do what he'd been wanting to do.

Angry llamas have a nasty habit
of spitting at those they do not like, and when
Albert judged Solomon to be near enough,
he would spit at him.

At precisely the same instant, Solomon,
with a shrill neigh of fury, would whip round
and lash out at Albert with his hind hooves,
trying to catch him on the chin. I never
saw either of them score – it was always
a goalless draw. Solomon's heels never
quite reached Albert, and Albert's spit
never quite hit Solomon.

But each lived in hope that one
day he'd succeed.

The Stowaway

ON A CRUISE MY WIFE AND I TOOK TO THE WEST
INDIES, there were about thirteen hundred
people – passengers and crew – aboard the
ship, and one pigeon.

It was a perfectly ordinary-looking
pigeon, bluish-grey and pink-legged, just like
any one of the thousands of birds you see in
city streets and squares.

But this was a very clever pigeon.

In no time at all it found out that not only
do people on cruise liners eat a lot – they also
spill and drop a lot of food on deck.

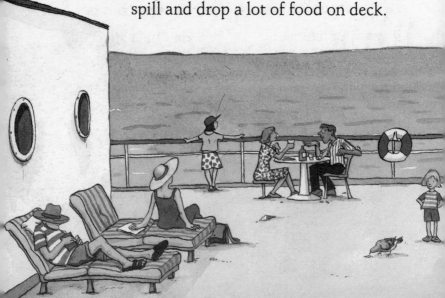

The pigeon made itself at home on the lido deck, where many of the passengers came to sit outside for breakfast and lunch. Every day, throughout these mealtimes, it strutted about underneath the tables, pecking up bits of food that had been dropped, sometimes on purpose. Some thoughtful person always put down an ashtray filled with fresh water.

All the way across the Atlantic, the pigeon ate and ate, until it couldn't stand, but lay on its stomach.

Eventually, after weeks of feasting, it was put ashore.

But I wouldn't mind betting that it stowed away again on the very next cruise liner that called there.

Dodo: Star of the Show

OUR MINIATURE RED WIRE-HAIRED DACHSHUND, Dodo, was born on a farm in west Wales, and from the moment we picked her up to bring her home with us, it was plain that she was a most unusual dog.

Though so young and so small, she was very self-possessed. The first of our animals that she met was a Great Dane. He bent his huge head to this midget. She looked up and wagged at him.

Some years later, when Dodo was about five, something happened that changed her life.

A television producer was looking for a presenter for a small slot on a children's programme. She needed someone who had

been a farmer and a teacher and wrote books
for children (that turned out to be me), and
who also owned a small, attractive dog
(that was Dodo).

Dodo and I must have made about fifty
little films.

Though I improved as time went on,
Dodo didn't need to: she was immediately
at home in front of the cameras. Not only did
she like people, so that she always got on very

well with the film crews, but she was always extremely likeable herself.

At first, the crew came often to our cottage, for we filmed a number of animals there or near by, and they always arrived promptly at nine o'clock on a Thursday morning.

By a quarter to nine each Thursday (and only on Thursdays,) Dodo would be waiting by the door for them to arrive and admire her.

Don't ask me how she knew. I don't know.

After a while Dodo began to be recognized in public. In London once, I suddenly heard some children crying, "Look! It's Dodo!" and they rushed up and made a fuss of her, which she loved; not because she was vain but because she was always so friendly to everyone.

And it wasn't only children who recognized her.

The guard of an Intercity train once came
to punch my ticket (and hers).

"Why," he said, "if it isn't Dodo!"

She was always the star of the show.

Joe Crow

THE LATEST ANIMAL IN MY LIFE is sitting on the wall below my study window as I write. Now and again he looks up with a bright, considering eye. He is a young crow, not long fledged. We call him Joe.

I first met Joe a week ago. He was hopping down the lane. "Can't you fly?" I said, and for an answer he did, not very well, but well enough to get onto my garden wall. A couple of hours later he was outside the back door, flapping his wings and opening his beak in a gesture that said plainly, "Feed me! Feed me!" Where his mother and father were, I don't know, but it was plain that I was expected to take their place.

Now Joe is always waiting for bits of soaked dog-meal. I feed them to him beside the

greenhouse. After he's
eaten, Joe goes up to the side
of the greenhouse, sees another Joe reflected,
and pecks angrily at it.

He's growing stronger and flying better
by the day. Not surprising really, because
our friends who live on the other side of the
lane (a hundred yards as the crow flies) tell
me that they are busy feeding a young crow
who keeps asking for food. And our next-door
neighbours say the same. No fool, Joe.

But we think of him as ours because
he spends each evening with us. We sit in the
garden, talking, and Joe sits
on the fence behind with his
head on one side, listening.
And at night he roosts
on our roof.

Postscript

REMEMBER DODO, THE STAR OF
THE SHOW? It might be nice, I'm
thinking now, to end with
a mention of another miniature
red wire-haired dachshund called Little Elsie,
who is sitting watching me.

Why? Because Little Elsie is Dodo's
grand-daughter.

She's quite a different character from her
granny – not as jolly and outgoing, less sure
of herself (though she's as
fierce as a lion when left in
charge of the car); in fact
not the film star type.

But the older Little Elsie grows – and she's really quite old now, though still very active – the more she gets to look like her grandmother. Her red coat has paled with age, her beard and moustache are fuller, her muzzle is grey.

And lately a funny thing has begun to happen. We keep calling Elsie by the wrong name. Several times a day, one or other of us will say, "Come along, Dodo" and along comes Little Elsie, wagging her tail and doing her special trick, which is to bare her teeth in a grin of pleasure.

Dick King-Smith (1922–2011) is one of the world's favourite children's book authors. He won the Guardian Children's Fiction Prize for *The Sheep-Pig* (filmed as *Babe*), was named Children's Book Author of the Year in 1991 and received the 1995 Children's Book Award for *Harriet's Hare*. His fiction titles for Walker include the much-loved Sophie series, *The Finger-Eater, Aristotle, The Twin Giants,* and *Lady Lollipop* and *Clever Lollipop.*

Anita Jeram has illustrated numerous children's books, including the worldwide best-selling *Guess How Much I Love You* (shortlisted for the Kurt Maschler Award and the Illustrated Children's Book of the Year Award), the *Guess How Much I Love You* Storybooks and *You're All My Favourites*, all by Sam McBratney. She also illustrated several books by Amy Hest, including *Little Chick* and *Kiss Good Night*. She lives in Northern Ireland.